The School of Life Guide to Modern Manners

First published in 2019 by The School of Life
First published in the USA in 2020
This paperback edition published in 2024
930 High Road, London, N12 9RT

Copyright © The School of Life 2019
Cover design by @marciamihotichstudio

Printed and bound by CPI Group (UK) Ltd, Croydon, CR0 4YY

All rights reserved. This book is sold subject to the condition that it shall not be resold, lent, hired out, or otherwise circulated without express prior consent of the publisher.

A proportion of this book has appeared online at www.theschooloflife.com/articles

Every effort has been made to contact the copyright holders of the material reproduced in this book. If any have been inadvertently overlooked, the publisher will be pleased to make restitution at the earliest opportunity.

The School of Life publishes a range of books on essential topics in psychological and emotional life, including relationships, parenting, friendship, careers, and fulfillment. The aim is always to help us to understand ourselves better—and thereby to grow calmer, less confused, and more purposeful. Discover our full range of titles, including books for children, here: www.theschooloflife.com/books

The School of Life also offers a comprehensive therapy service, which complements, and draws upon, our published works: www.theschooloflife.com/therapy

www.theschooloflife.com

ISBN 978-1-916753-05-1

10 9 8 7 6 5 4 3 2 1

The School of Life Guide to Modern Manners

Navigating the anxieties of social life

The School of Life

Contents

	Introduction	7
1	How to Tell When You Are Being a Bore	11
2	How to Write an Effective Thank You Letter	17
3	How to Choose a Good Present	23
4	How to Approach Strangers at a Party	29
5	What to Do at Parties If You Hate Small Talk	33
6	How to Shake Someone Off at a Party	39
7	How to Win People Over	45
8	Whether, and How Much, to Praise	49
9	How to Successfully Disappoint Someone Socially	55
10	How to Be Comfortable on Your Own in Public	61
11	How to Deal with Upsets in Service Situations	67
12	How to Become Someone People Will Confide In	73
13	How to Talk to a Bereaved Acquaintance	77
14	How to Spill a Drink down Your Front—and Survive	83
15	How to Deal with the Subtext	89
16	How to Stop Worrying Whether or Not They Like You	95
17	How to Be a Good Guest	101
18	How to Tell Someone They Have Spinach between Their Teeth	107
19	How to Make People Feel Good about Themselves	113
20	How to Face Social Catastrophe	119

Introduction

Social life is full of minor but acute dilemmas. We get stuck at a gathering with someone unusually tedious and wonder how to move on without causing offense. In the course of introducing one friend to another, we realize that we have forgotten one of their names. We run into a disappointed ex while on an early date with a new partner. We spill a Bloody Mary across a host's absorbent pale couch.

The dilemmas are—at one level—pathetically insignificant. But they sit astride some of the largest and most serious themes in social existence: how to pursue our own agenda for happiness while at the same time honoring the sensitivities and wishes of others; how to convey goodwill with sincerity; how to repair damage caused by inattention or self-centeredness; how to be kind without being supine or sentimental.

These dilemmas fall into a category that once belonged to the field of etiquette or manners. The modern age has generally had enough of manners, equating them with an aristocratic era of subterfuge and fakeness; we are advised to go with our feelings and tell it the way it really is.

But the result, in practice, is that we are often confused as to how to act around others and discharge our obligations to them. What follows are twenty case studies that focus on common social dilemmas and our possible responses to them, that together try to contribute to a philosophy of graceful and generous conduct. Manners are far from negligible fancies; they stand at the day-to-day end of a hugely grand and dignified mission: the creation of a kinder world.

1
How to Tell When You Are Being a Bore

Some of the reason why we end up being inadvertently rude to people is that they are so polite with us—in a way that doesn't give us sufficient information as to whether we might be inconveniencing or boring them.

It can at points be hard to tell whether what we are saying is really of any interest to those we are addressing. Few people—other than our partner in a bad mood or our adolescent child—will ever directly cut us short and announce that they find us dull. It is as a result all too easy to develop an impression of our own compelling nature. If we were to ask our interlocutor, "Am I boring you?" we can be certain that the one answer we would never receive is: "Well, since you ask, yes you are rather." If we choose to wait until people fall asleep while we're recounting an anecdote or check their phone as we get to the punchline of our joke, it will be too late. Our reputation as a windbag will long ago have been sealed.

Fortunately, most of what people need to tell us does not have to be directly stated; the evolution of a civilization can be measured by the scope of its dictionary of unspoken signals. The clue to another's interest lies not in their overt declarations but in their degree of responsiveness to our words. We can gauge interest by studying how closely and logically another's questions follow on from our statements; how fast their replies come; how invested they seem in their emphases; whether their eyes meet ours when we stress a point; and the degree of elasticity and benevolence in their smile. To a trained observer, an urgent cry—"I need to go to bed now"—can be communicated by nothing more brutal or direct than a gaze at the overhead smoke alarm that is held a fraction too long or a "That's wonderful" that lacks a minute but critical dose of wonder.

It is mostly easy enough to note the cues; when we ignore them, it isn't that we aren't receiving them, but that we are somehow opting not to register them—

and we are not doing so for a poignant reason: because we cannot bear to imagine that we might be boring, because the idea of not belonging sufficiently deeply in another's life is untenable; because we are unreconciled to the fundamental loneliness of existence and the tragic disjuncture between what we want from others and what they may be prepared to provide. We grow deaf from the rigidity of our need, not from any basic failure of sensitivity.

Somewhere along the line the idea of not pleasing someone conversationally may turn from a reasonable risk into a prospective catastrophe that must be manically warded off. We become wilfully oblivious; we give up seeking to delight and settle instead on the more modest hope of not being actively thrown out. The insult to our self-love that we read into another's bored reaction feels too great, and our resources to deal with it too slim for us to take in the meaning of the long pauses and wandering eyes. We overlook the cues because what they indicate to our unconscious minds isn't the relatively innocuous thought that the other wants to go to bed; they become embroiled in a deeper story about our self-worth: we take them to indicate that we are fundamentally displeasing, that we deserve our isolation or that we are hateful wretches.

The best guarantee of not boring others is—therefore—the development of an internal robustness that can allow us to withstand the idea that we naturally do have tedious sides, as everyone does. The interesting person can acknowledge that losing someone's attention is a setback, but not an exceptional sign of damnation.

To develop a more benevolent picture of what it means occasionally to bore, it can help to study the responses of parents to their small children, for there are no better examples of the easy coexistence of boredom with love. To a parent, their 4-year-old child will be at once the most loveable creature they have ever met—and, by a long way, especially in their conversation, the most tedious. Even outside of parenthood, we are all endowed with surprisingly rich capacities to love someone and at the same time to find them extremely wearing. It does not, as the bore mistakenly ends up thinking, need to be a choice between love and interest on the one hand and tedium and loathing on the other.

To skirt the danger of being a full-blown bore, we should foster the courage to imagine that we might sometimes, without anything too awful being meant by this, be just such a thing.

2
How to Write an Effective Thank You Letter

Life continually requires that we write down a few words of thanks: for vacations, meals, presents, or parties. However, too often, our messages end up flat or unconvincing; we say that the dinner was "wonderful," the present "brilliant," and the vacation "the best ever," all of which may be true while failing to get at what truly touched or moved us.

To render our messages more effective, we might take a lesson from an unexpected quarter: the history of art. Many paintings and poems are in effect a series of thank you notes to parts of the world. They are thank yous for the sunset in springtime, a river valley at dawn, the last days of fall, or the face of a loved one.

What distinguishes great from mediocre art is in large measure the level of detail with which the world has been studied. A talented artist is, first and foremost, someone who takes us into the specifics of the reasons why an experience or place felt valuable. They don't merely tell us that spring is "nice"; they zero in on the particular contributing factors to this niceness: leaves that have the softness of a newborn's hands, the contrast between a warm sun and a sharp breeze, the plaintive cry of baby blackbirds. The more the poet moves from generalities to specifics, the more the scene comes alive in our minds. The same holds true in painting. A great painter goes beneath a general impression of pleasure in order to select and emphasize the truly attractive features of the landscape: They show the sunlight filtering through the leaves of the trees and reflecting off a pool of water in the road; they draw attention to the craggy upper slopes of a mountain or the way a sequence of ridges and valleys open up in the distance. They've asked themselves with unusual rigor what it is that they particularly appreciated about a scene and faithfully transcribed their most salient impressions.

Some of the reason why great artists are rare is that our minds are not well set up to understand why we feel as we do. We register our emotions in broad strokes and derive an overall sense of our moods long before we grasp the basis upon which they rest. We are bad at traveling upstream from our impressions to their source; it feels frustrating to have to ask too directly what was really pleasing about a present or why exactly a person seemed charming to have dinner with.

But we can be confident that if our minds have been affected, the reasons why they have been so will be lodged somewhere in our consciousness as well, waiting to be uncovered with deftness and patience. We stand to realize that it wasn't so much that the food was "delicious," but that the potatoes in particular had an intriguing rosemary and garlic flavor to them. A friend wasn't just "nice"; they brought a hugely sensitive and generous tone to bear in asking us what it had been like for us in adolescence after our dad died. And the camera wasn't just a "great present"; it has an immensely satisfying rubbery grip and a reassuringly clunky shutter sound that evokes a sturdier, older world. The details will be there, waiting for us to catch them through our mental sieve.

Praise works best the more specific it can be. We know this in love; the more a partner can say what it is they appreciate about us, the more real their affection will feel. It is when they've studied the shape of our fingers, when they've recognized and appreciated the quirks of our character, when they've clocked the words we like or the way we end a phone call that the praise starts to count. The person who has given a dinner party or sent us a present is no different. They too hunger for praise in its specific rather than general forms. We don't have to be great artists to send effective thank you notes: we just need to locate and hold on tightly to two or three highly detailed reasons for our gratitude.

3
How to Choose a Good Present

One of the reasons it can be so hard to buy other adults presents is that we haven't at some level quite factored in that we are now all grown-ups. Presents were (probably) a deeply special part of our childhoods. We anticipated them eagerly, depended on them almost exclusively—and could be driven to either paroxysms of joy or of sadness by their quality.

But a lot has changed since then. Chiefly, all of us now have our own money. Anything that our friends are badly likely to want, they will either be able to buy for themselves—or we won't be able to afford to buy it for them.

This isn't to say that other adults don't have any requirements; it's merely that what they seek from us is largely psychological rather than material in nature. Our adult friends do—just like children—need us to offer them things that they can't get for themselves. But, unlike children, these are not things we could ever buy in a store: they want encouragement and compassion, they want to be listened to with understanding and sympathy; they want someone to fathom the agonies of their relationships and their struggles at work. They crave our kindness, care, and interest. They want us to be active in their lives, to forgive them for their follies, and to appreciate their strengths.

The sense of despair that hangs over the process of choosing a present stems from our background awareness of how hard it will be to ever successfully identify a material object out in the world that could properly quench a sincere need in another adult. Though once or twice in our lives, we may hit on just the thing, the chances of locating such an object are too minuscule to be statistically relevant—as our own attics and closets, filled as they are with the fruits of others' misguided good intentions, poignantly attest.

We would be better off facing up maturely to the hurdle we face. We cannot hope to guess with any degree of specificity at the objects still missing from the lives of our friends. At the same time, there is no question that we should and must bring presents, for we are all too fragile to believe in love without a wrapped box to underpin our claims.

The solution lies in toning down our ambitions. We won't be able to determine the subtler contours of the gaps in the material lives of those we love. And yet it is still open to us to offer the kinds of objects we know they will need, not because we can peer into their souls, but because they are human. We should concentrate our efforts on buying them somewhat above-average examples of the "material" of daily life: scissors, rulers, elastic bands, pencils, notepads, olive oil, salt, nail clippers, earplugs, mineral water, dish soap … the things we can be guaranteed to need and always to lack. By investing in slightly higher quality versions of these staples—for example, tracking down one of the very best kinds of dust pans or cans of tuna—we will be emphasizing our degree of care. But the very obviousness of the present is a way of owning up to the dilemma we are up against and of signaling with grace that our real role in our friends' lives is of an emotional, not a practical, nature.

Showing up with a particularly large and tempting loaf of bread or a luxurious collection of paper clips, we are implicitly declaring the impossibility of fathoming the genuine material gaps in our friends' lives—while taking on board our true responsibility toward them, which is and always was: to love them.

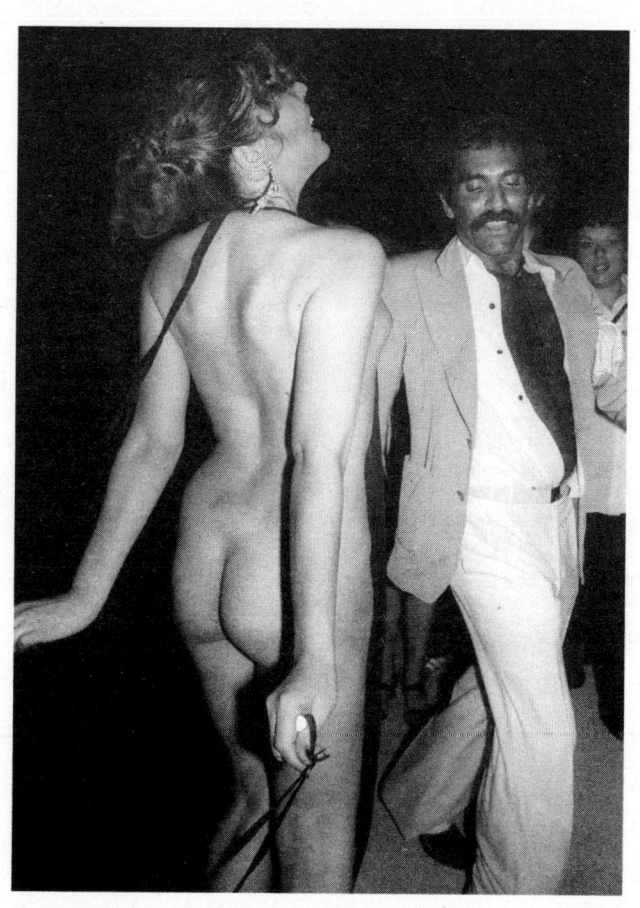

4
How to Approach Strangers at a Party

A party at the house of a friend, eleven o'clock, on a still-warm evening. A yard away from you, a group of people are chatting animatedly. Someone is telling an anecdote—it might be something about a subway ride they took or the mishaps on someone's bicycle—and their companions break in occasionally with rich laughter and stories of their own. The group as a whole seem confident and attractive and the main narrator especially so. But there may as well be a high solid brick wall between you and them. There is resolutely no way you could ever move in to say hello. You smile your characteristic weak, loser's smile, pretend to study the bookshelf—and leave the gathering ten minutes later.

Much of the advice provided by books and guides concerns what we might say in these circumstances. It could be better to start somewhere else: with what we should think. Chronic shyness is a guess about what other people are like. Though it doesn't feel like it when it has flooded us, shyness reflects a rationally founded assessment as to the nature and intentions of other members of our species. It is not a chemical imbalance or an impulse, it's a philosophy, albeit a deeply unhelpful one.

Its essential assumption is that other people are self-sufficient, that they do not lack for company, that they are not alone with anything, that they understand all they need to know—and that they do not share in any of our frailties, hesitations, secret longings, or confusions. This echoes, in an adult form, the assumptions a child might make of their teacher, a competent stern grown-up who appears never to have been young, silly, tender, or interested in a pillow fight.

This lack of faith in the humanity of others is a natural tendency of our minds. We go by external cues—and therefore come to assume that we are living among superior, metal-plated cyborgs rather than fragile, water-filled uncertain entities. We cannot believe that most of what we know of our own minds, especially the self-doubt, the anxiety, and the sadness, exists in strangers too.

We're slow to convert this crucial insight into a social strategy, into a confidence-inducing knowledge that others must also, as we do, harbor warmth, longing, curiosity, and sorrow—the ingredients from which new friendships are built. A seemingly happily married person might have a lot of agony around the course of their relationship; a pugnacious sportsman might suffer from chronic anxiety and shame; a CEO might have vivid memories of their struggles and a lot of space in their imagination for people whose careers have yet to take off. A very intellectual person might—internally—be longing for a new friend who could patiently encourage them to dance (or forgive their inept gyrations). Our error is to suppose that the way a person seems is the whole of who they are: Our anxiety closes off the core fact that we are all much more approachable than we appear.

The key to self-belief—and the mindset to talk to strangers successfully—doesn't lie in strenuously insisting on our own merits; its source is a more accurate and less forbidding mode of imagining the inner lives, and especially the inner troubles, of others.

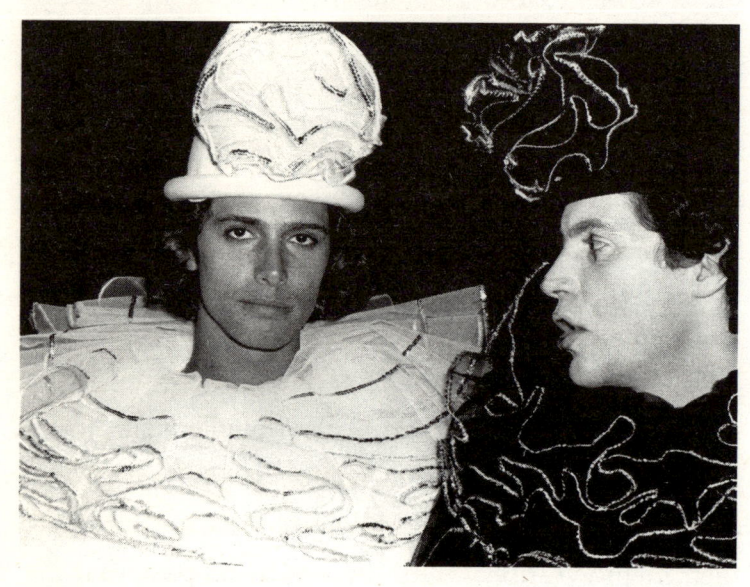

5
What to Do at Parties If You Hate Small Talk

A lot of discomfort about going to social engagements is rooted in what can sound like a rather high-minded concern: a hatred of small talk. We can develop a dread of parties because we know how likely we are to end up wedged into conversations about the weather, parking, traffic, or the way we plan to spend the forthcoming holidays—when there could be so many deeper and more dignified topics to address: the future of humanity, the fate of the nation, or the melancholy state of our hearts. We resent parties for holding up an ideal of community and dialogue while trapping us in unproductive and insincere banter; for making us more lonely than we ever would be in our own homes.

But we are perhaps misunderstanding what small talk is for, what it could be in our hands, and how we might gently find an exit from its more airless corners. Small talk exists for a noble reason: it is designed to prevent hurt. It provides us with a rich source of information so that we can safely ascertain the frame of mind of our interlocutor—and therefore gauge what more in-depth topics of conversation might safely be broached. The German philosopher Arthur Schopenhauer once darkly reminded us that we should always remember, when meeting new people, that they might be only a few steps away from wanting to grab a weapon and end their own lives. A few moments of small talk can give us the signals we need to find out who we have on our hands; it lends us time to circle intimacy from on high before determining where we might wish to land.

Furthermore, a rigid hatred of small talk overlooks that it isn't ever the subject matter per se that determines the profundity of a conversation. There are ways of talking about death that are trivial and ways of addressing the weather that feel significant. A truly deep mind can exercise itself as much on the game of a child as on the puzzles of philosophy—and it is unfortunate snobbery (mistaking the outward label for

John Constable, *Cloud Study: Stormy Sunset*, 1821–1822

the inner content) to discount a topic merely because it has never featured in erudite academic curricula.

We should take inspiration from how many great artists have based their work around what were, at heart, versions of "small talk." In the early 1820s, the English artist John Constable painted fifty studies of the clouds above Hampstead Heath in London, finding extraordinary beauty and complexity in the ever-changing quiet aerial drama above him. Buddhism teaches us that, to those gifted enough to see properly, the whole world can be found in a single grain of sand. We should perceive no insult in an occasional call to glimpse the grandest themes through the lens of small talk.

The skilled conversationalist doesn't insist that atmospheric or traffic conditions or where a person has been at the coast are inherently unworthy of discussion. They know that what a person feels about a cloudy afternoon might be a highway to their soul or that their experiences around parking might provide clues as to their attitudes to authority or their relations with their parents. They are not put off by having to work with humble matter; they will make use of whatever is to hand.

The fear of small talk reflects a worry, hugely understandable and with roots in childhood experience, that we will be unable to influence the flow of a conversation, that we will be the victims of the obsession or pettiness of others—and that conversation is fundamentally a natural, organic occurrence which happens to us but cannot be created by us; it may at points be very engaging, at other points hugely frustrating; but the outcome is not ours to determine. We feel that when a person says something, we must invariably respond in a similar way: one anecdote needs to be followed by another; if someone has a story about a booking confusion at a hotel, the other must chip in with a corollary.

But in truth, we have far more conversational agency than this implies; it is almost always in our power to raise more intimate or profound follow-up questions. And we can do so with the confidence that few of us are ever committed to remaining on the surface; we just don't know how to descend to the depths. An individual who is currently talking at puzzling length about an airline meal has also inevitably been disappointed in love, had bouts of despair, tried to make sense of a difficult parent, felt confused about their direction—and will be longing, at some level, therefore, to stop talking about cheese crackers and share the contents of their heart.

The confident conversationalist does not take fright at small talk and others' occasional apparently firm attachment to it. They know that minor themes need only ever be the first, understandable, and never insulting steps toward the sincerity and intimacy we all crave at heart.

6
How to Shake Someone Off at a Party

At a party where people have come to flirt and hunt for partners, or at a gathering where fledgling entrepreneurs meet with prospective investors, two individuals who (it quickly emerges) can offer each other very little, fall into a conversation. Out of a sense of dutiful politeness, they ask each other about their work or share news of a mutual acquaintance. But the conversation soon starts to drag and (perhaps for both of them) to feel a little desperate, given how rich in opportunities the evening could be: All around them are people with whom they might restart their romantic lives or who could help them realize their entrepreneurial schemes. And yet they cannot find any decent way to escape an agonizing discussion about office software or an exam at college a decade before.

Knowing how to exit a conversation elegantly is as important a skill as to know how to begin one. But what may hold us back isn't first and foremost an absence of the right kinds of lines, it's a discomfort about our own motives. Our ineptness is often just a symptom of a lack of conviction. We can't confidently bring the conversation to a close because we do not, at some level, believe that it could be right to leave behind a friendly soul for the sake of something as low as a search for love (and sex) or money. Our hesitancy reflects an adherence to an underlying philosophy of niceness by which we feel profoundly hesitant around our own appetites for seduction or networking.

But we should, within reason, recover confidence in the dignity of what we are trying to do. There is nothing inherently shameful in attempting to locate someone with whom we might exchange flirtatious banter and in time, if things were to go exceptionally well, begin a relationship and one day start a family. Nor is there anything categorically mean-minded about trying to engage with someone who might invest in the next financing round of our business and help us achieve our entrepreneurial vision.

An end to our tongue-tiedness should begin with a renewed faith that we can be an eminently good person and—at a moment replete with opportunity—sharply intent on getting rid of anyone who might stand in our way. The opposite of selfishness is not a lack of agency; it is a forthright acceptance of the importance of occasionally foregrounding our own priorities. We can be a very kind parent and at moments tell our child that we are not in the mood to play a game with them; a good lover and not agree with every scheme our partner proposes—and a kindly soul and selective about whom we talk to at parties.

Our adequate development depends on our ability to carve out periods in which our own needs predominate. Later, when our romantic hopes have been catered for and our business is established, there will be plenty of time to chat in expansive and serendipitous ways to anyone who crosses our path. But for now, we should learn to make our excuses and head off into the crowd.

To do so as graciously as possible, we should reframe our intentions so that they apply to our conversational partner rather than to ourselves. We might apologetically exclaim: "I really wouldn't want to monopolize you for any more of the evening!" Or, more playfully, we might say: "Your future husband or wife isn't going to forgive me for delaying you meeting them any further!" What we should avoid is the sort of frustration with the situation that leads us to being overtly rude or puzzling. We should not ask our friend if they'd like another drink and then never return; or claim to be exhausted and headed for bed but then re-emerge at the bar two hours later. We should make ourselves at home with what we really want and adopt the confident yet kindly tone of those who know they can remain good people and yet be still entitled to wander cleanly off and talk to someone else.

7
How to Win People Over

It's an irony of social life that what often holds us back from connecting with others is the sense that we are not impressive enough to merit their attention: Our careers are not sufficiently elevated, our lives are too filled with setbacks, and our mood is overly melancholy.

But in taking a step back because of this, we are misunderstanding a basic law of interpersonal psychology: that, with a few caveats in mind, people like to hear of the sadness of others. Learning that someone else is in pain, finds things difficult, has made a mess of their work, is unhappy in love, and is sometimes very anxious and melancholy is not—generally—appalling; it is hugely reassuring. It breaks our sense of isolation.

It lifts the burden of having to be respectable, successful, and "normal." It is the beginning of friendship and warmth.

Conversely, it is deeply upsetting to hear that someone is in a flawless relationship or is delighted with their job. We are all—understandably—far too unhappy to respond with joy to the good news of others. Misery charms.

What people are afraid of is not vulnerability, but obligation; the requirement that—on account of having been an audience to a problem—they now have to look after a sufferer on a long-term basis, appease them, soothe them, perhaps bail them out and quieten their sobs. This is legitimately frightening.

But there isn't any necessary connection between the revelation of vulnerability and the birth of an obligation. We can sketch out the disasters that afflict us without holding our audience to ransom or manipulating them through guilt. We can lay out our sores and mishaps with a winning gallows humor; we can cast ourselves as the unwitting central figure in a macabre black comedy. We can invite recognition without exacting pity. We can suggest that we are both falling apart and eminently holding it together. Few things are socially more seductive than a glimpse of weakness borne with strength.

It is tragic that we should spend so much of our social lives trying to impress others when it is really the judicious revelation of weakness that builds intimacy and turns strangers into friends.

8
Whether, and How Much, to Praise

Sometimes, a surprisingly positive thought flits through our minds at the idea of a friend or acquaintance: one of them strikes us as really very funny in company, managing to deliver lines with forensically aimed deadpan humor; another seems exceptionally kind; a third has done so well in a challenging and noble field of work …

We might like to say something to them, sharing the warm regard we have for them in explicit terms. But a reserve tends to hold us back. There can seem no context or precedent for interrupting the flow of regular banter in order to share our admiration for them. We risk sounding too "heavy" or fake, as if we might in a sinister way be trying to move things on beyond just a friendship, or were about to ask them for something huge in return, like a loan or letter of recommendation. Because our societies are sharply primed to the dangers of narcissism, offering praise can seem as if it might inflame our friend's ego, hyping up their self-regard beyond safe levels—and so damaging the very character we had come to admire. Surely the friend already knows full well what's good about them: a reminder will only herald an unseemly egotism. It generally seems best to keep our warm thoughts about our friends for the only occasion where it is entirely legitimate to divulge them: their funerals.

Yet our reserve is deeply misplaced. For a start, far from being at risk of thinking too well of ourselves, most of us fight a daily battle not to fall into self-loathing and despair. We are constantly burdened by a sense of our own inadequacy. We don't think we are witty or particularly intelligent; we are painfully aware of our confusions and failings; we fear we come across as ridiculous; we don't like ourselves very much and don't assume others would be particularly enthusiastic about us either.

In this context, a few words of praise—far from tipping us into egomania—may be what separates us from a lapse into depression and self-suspicion. Though it can be easy to presume otherwise from the outside, we ourselves don't know that our dinner was any good, that our jokes have been funny, that our kindness has been noted, or that our presence is wanted. Because no one else does very much straightforward reassurance, our friends are likely never to have heard anyone praise them directly for a long time. We might assume that the funny person has been flattered to the skies or that the accomplished artist has been given all the reassurance they could need, and that our appreciation would therefore be only one more slightly unnecessary bunch of flowers at the foot of the monument to their ego. But we underestimate how parched most of us are of praise, not because we are insatiable egotists, but because social life doesn't encourage or provide occasions when praise can freely be shared.

Lovers are meant to shower their partners with positive regard (which is partly why romantic love occupies such an unfair space in our imaginations); but friends take each other's good sides slightly for granted. We assume it is enough just to be nice—and that friends will in this way get the message about how we feel about them, forgetting that we are all far too self-doubting not to assume the worst.

We should carve out regular moments when praise can be given; we should hold back the ordinary flow of dialogue in order to introduce a few sentences that explicitly point out what is good and admirable about those we care about. We shouldn't hold back out of timidity or fear of the other's nascent arrogance. We aren't at risk of creating monsters, we're saving people from the monstrous depredations of self-doubt—and enabling them to have enough confidence to keep doing good in the world.

9
How to Successfully Disappoint Someone Socially

There are many occasions in social life when we have to let people down. A work commitment means we're going to have to cancel dinner. A more exciting prospect has come our way for Thursday evening. We're too busy to join friends on their vacation as we'd hoped. We're exhausted and want to leave the party early.

But the thought of having to disappoint someone whose good opinion of us we value can be a source of so much anxiety, we may end up unwittingly adding rudeness and offense to the basic frustration we impose on others. As in politics, it can be the cover-up, not the original mishap, that does the damage.

Unsure that the brute information (we have to leave; we're not going to be there) is forgivable, we try to remove its sting through overly ornate explanations, each one more baroque and complicated than the last. It's not just that a work meeting threatens to overrun, it's also that our car hasn't come back from repairs, that the babysitter is ill, that our boss will be in Milan that week, that we have to compile a report before Monday and that the IT system has swallowed our emails.

Or else, guilty at the superficial nature of our priorities, we may get drawn to highly tragic and somber explanations for our no-show that retain perhaps only a toehold on the truth: Our grandmother is extremely ill with what they suspect is cholera; an uncle has had what seems to be a stroke; an old school friend is close to suicidal ...

Or, unable to correctly gauge the impact of our absence on others, we presumptuously assume a pivotal role in the proceedings and proffer overblown reassurances or moist-eyed enquiries as to our friend's wellbeing in the wake of our news. We ask in a soft and careful voice if they will really be OK to go ahead with dinner without us there to support them? We counsel that we sincerely think they can still have a good time at the beach without us. We sound very concerned and worried about how they will cope without us, as if we had been entrusted with an especially vulnerable chick with a broken wing (that we've just ourselves smashed).

Or else, worried that nothing can ever be made good, we enter into a nihilistic mindset and become pre-emptively aggressive, acting out with others what we fear they may do to us.

In order to become more skillful rejectors, we need to develop the courage and sangfroid of our own selfishness. What the person we're rejecting needs are the facts, an apology, some space to get over their hurt, and some time to rejig their plans; nothing more. What they don't need are layers of explanations that either feel untrue or are so serious as not to leave them any room to mourn their own social loss.

Nor do they need excessive concern on the part of the person who has hurt them, with doe-eyed enquiries that humiliatingly emphasize their dependence on the very person who has rejected them.

We need to be terse, focused—and ready to accept that we won't for a time be thought very nice by someone to whom we haven't been very nice. We need to send B not A:

A:

I know you've put ever so much work into your party on Thursday—and I know how much you're relying on me to be there, but (this is so sad!), Uncle Chris has just come down with an inflammation of the larynx, I'm going to have to move apartment, David is flying in from LA and my boss is unwell, which means I sadly, sadly—yikes!!—don't think I can make it. But will you be OK? Is there anything I can do to help you beforehand? Can I come and clean up after? I love you so much. I'm thinking of you and hope you'll manage without me.

B:

I'm so sorry, something's come up. I'm going to have to be a pain and let you down on Thursday night. I apologize deeply. Please forgive me. I'll do far better by you next time.

10
How to Be Comfortable on Your Own in Public

We're spending a few days on business in a town where we know no one. It's dinner time and, feeling claustrophobic in our hotel room, we wander the main streets looking for a place to eat. The bars and restaurants are filled with loving couples and animated groups of friends. We gingerly enter a diner but, as we take in the warmth and convivial atmosphere, we are struck by acute self-consciousness. We blush crimson and clumsily turn to leave before an approaching waiter has had the chance to offer us a seat. We eventually find a dried-out sandwich at the station kiosk, which we eat furtively on a park bench near some loitering pigeons.

Eating alone in public can be one of the great hurdles of psychological life. It can be an exceptional trial because it forces us to wrestle with a set of thoughts that, for most of our lives, we successfully push to the back of consciousness: that we are in essence an unacceptable being, tainted from birth, an outcast, non-specifically diseased, unattractive to others, an object of quiet ridicule or open mockery, undeserving of love and sinful to the core. We may not have this explicit thesis in mind as we decline to sit down by ourselves, but the scale of our embarrassment speaks of a searing latent suspicion of our own being.

How loveable we feel as adults is, in large measure, the result of how we have been looked after by a few significant figures in childhood. No one is born with a capacity to love and endure themselves on their own; we learn to soothe and care for ourselves by first experiencing the tender gaze of others, and then internalizing their reassurance and kindness, replaying it to ourselves in isolated circumstances down the years. The lucky ones among us, those with no compunction about ordering a meal at a table for one, must—somewhere in the distant past—have grown secure through others' admiration, by which they now ward off suspicions that the head waiter is sniggering and the couple in the corner are teasing them. When they were perhaps not much larger than a pillow, they were lent a powerful sense that they had a right to exist, that they were an asset to the world, that others should be pleased to see them, which means that now, even when the caregivers are long gone, they can imagine that the laughter from the next table is innocent and that they deserve to be brought another basket of bread and the evening paper.

But the less fortunate among us have no such emotional blanket. Whatever our accomplishments or status, we are never far from a sense that everyone is mocking and would have good reason to harm us. We need, with a conscious effort, to do what others were taught to do by their histories. One side of the mind needs to comfort the other—must make the reassuring noises we never natively received, must soothe us because no one else ever did. Although we're on our own in the restaurant at the moment, we must strive to hold on to a picture of the rest of our lives: two days ago, we were laughing with our friends (of whom we have some great examples), tomorrow we'll be in intense discussion with some colleagues: we have been loved and held tightly in others' arms before. We're on our own right now, but we're not social outcasts after all.

We should remember—along the way—how little anyone ever thinks of us, in the best possible sense. People are for the most part gloriously indifferent to each other. They don't spend their time plotting and hating; they simply don't care. The person cracking a joke with a group of friends has not rerouted their evening to mock us. The attractive individual deep in conversation with a companion isn't speculating about how isolated and ugly we are. Those are voices in our heads, not theirs.

Edward Hopper, *Automat*, 1927

We should take comfort too from the idea that there is at points a distinct dignity and grandeur to being an outsider, to not always being part of the pack, to taking time to step outside the normal social flow to consider humanity from an oblique solitary angle. The temporarily friendless and isolated person has privileges and the possibility for insight denied to those always surrounded by the easy chatter of acquaintances. The great champion of the lonely diner, the American painter Edward Hopper, knew how to lend appropriate prestige to those who are on the outside, who can nurture ideas not sanctioned by the crowd, whose loneliness deepens their soul and may make others long for their friendship. The central figure in *Automat* is far from an object of pity; she is a center of quiet depth and insight. We might yearn to sit with rather than feel sorry for her.

11
How to Deal with Upsets in Service Situations

We're in a restaurant and a waiter spills a glass of water over our jacket; we arrive at a hotel and are informed at reception that our room won't be ready for another four hours; the airline has mislaid our reservation and we'll have to take a later flight …

We're aware of possible mature responses to such incidents, but only too often, we throw grace aside, make bitter remarks—or start shouting.

Our loss of composure isn't simply a question of manners, it has to do with a background sense of what we deserve and how much we hate ourselves.

One of the most fundamental paths to remaining calm and kind around frustrating people is the power to hold on, even in very challenging situations, to a distinction between what someone does—and what they mean to do.

In law, the difference is enshrined in the contrasting concepts of murder and manslaughter. The result may be the same—the body is inert in a pool of blood—but we collectively feel it makes a huge difference what the perpetrator's intentions were. Motives are crucial. Yet unfortunately, when we lack a solid sense of ourselves, we can fail to perceive what the motives are likely to be behind many of the incidents that upset us. We see intention where there was none and escalate and confront when no strenuous or agitated responses are warranted. And we do so for a touching psychological reason: self-hatred. The less we like ourselves, the more we will appear in our own eyes to be plausible targets for mockery and harm. Why would a drill have started up outside, just as we were settling down to work? Why is the room service breakfast not arriving, even though we will have to be in a meeting very soon? Why would the phone operator be taking so long to find our details? Because there is—logically enough—a plot against us. Because we are appropriate targets for these kinds of things, because we are the sort of people against whom disruptive drilling is legitimately likely to be directed: because it's what we deserve.

When we carry an excess of self-disgust around with us, operating just below the radar of conscious awareness, we'll constantly seek confirmation from the wider world that we really are the worthless people we take ourselves to be. The expectation is almost always set in childhood, where someone close to us is likely to have left us feeling dirty and culpable—and as a result, we now travel through society assuming the worst, not because it is necessarily true (or pleasant) to do so, but because it feels familiar; and because we are the prisoners of past patterns we haven't yet understood.

To recover our composure, we must learn to be aware of our tendency to draw the cruellest picture of other people because, at heart, we feel cruel toward ourselves. We might learn to behave with other adults the way we spontaneously behave with small children. These children sometimes behave in stunningly frustrating ways: They scream at the person who is looking after them, angrily push away a bowl of animal pasta, throw away something you have just fetched for them. But we rarely feel personally agitated or wounded by their behavior. And the reason is that we don't assign a negative motive or mean intention to them.

We are robust enough not to take it personally. We reach around for the most benevolent interpretations. We don't think they are doing it in order to upset us because we are wretched. We probably think that they are getting a bit tired, or their gums are sore, or they are upset by the arrival of a younger sibling. We've got a large repertoire of alternative explanations ready in our heads—and none of these lead us to panic.

We should do the same with adults. We should imagine the source of problems that drive a person in a service situation to behave disrespectfully toward a customer. It almost certainly isn't anything to do specifically with us; probably it was a genuine error, or the manager is upset about something that happened in their relationship or is worried about money or is in physical pain … and we are the nearest target. We need to reimagine the lives of others and guess at the turmoil, disappointment, worry, and sadness in people who may outwardly appear merely aggressive or rude. We need to be patient with those who frustrate us most by accepting that, despite our lingering feelings of low self-worth, it is very seldom really anything to do with us.

12
How to Become Someone People Will Confide In

It is a mark of character to be thought of as someone that others can safely confide in; there is a high degree of empathy, generosity, and open-mindedness implied in being the person that friends instinctively turn to when everything has gone dark.

But we may come to realize that, despite our best intentions, often others do not quite see us in this way. If we ask them directly what the matter is, they try to look cheerful and insist that everything is fine. We know it can't be, but nor do they seem inclined to open up to us. We end up lonely and a little helpless.

There are plenty of good reasons why people tend to show extreme care before opening up. A confidant may turn out to be patronizing, alarmist, sentimental, panic-inducing, or moralistic. The dangers of humiliation can be acute. To dare to confide, we need a strong feeling that our companion is going to be unreservedly understanding, gentle, and kindly. But even if we feel ready to be all these things, how do we signal our capacities properly to others?

The almost touchingly obvious method is via direct assertion. "Don't worry, I won't judge," or simply, "You can tell me, I'm very understanding." But kind though such statements may be, they don't generally help because they don't touch the core fear that—whatever we say—we may still turn out to be disturbed by, or hostile to, the details of actual revelations.

The more skilled approach requires a greater degree of courage on our part. It involves regularly admitting to something difficult and troubling and rather shameful about ourselves. It's by letting others know something of our own vulnerabilities that we free them up to share some of the things they are terrified of admitting in their lives. Our revelation proves far better than a headline statement that we are reliable because we know from the inside what it's like to carry a dreadful secret and to feel frightened of another person's reaction to it. We're demonstrating a crucial idea: that we won't turn on them because we've trusted them not to turn on us.

The process of building up trust often functions in an incremental way: we reveal a small and not too awful fact about ourselves, and the other then starts to share a little of what's going on for them. From there, we take a bolder step of admitting to something more significantly awkward: something we know could be seen as really not very acceptable. We're inviting the other to follow us in turn and to feel secure in opening their hearts yet wider.

The underlying idea is that in order to demonstrate our position as an empathetic receiver of confidences, we have to show our broken and flawed sides: we've failed, so another can tell us of their failure; we've been hurt, so they can admit to being hurt; we've done very stupid things, so we're not going to turn against those who have also been at points very silly.

To be a good companion, it isn't enough simply to be polite or to commiserate. We need to take a risk. We need to give our friends something they could use against us—so that they can feel safe in giving us something we might use against them. Under the umbrella of mutually assured destruction, real trust and friendship can flourish.

13
How to Talk to a Bereaved Acquaintance

However abstractly committed we are to being kind and helping people out when they suffer, one of the hardest of all social situations is when we are called upon to say a few words to an acquaintance who has recently been bereaved. The demand can so frighten and discomfit us, we may try to do everything to avoid it—or if we can't, we may fall into a panic that renders us shifty, peculiar, and strangely rude as well.

We get into a turmoil for a range of almost logical reasons. Chiefly, we're aware of the enormous contrast between how little we know the bereaved person and the magnitude of what has befallen them. How can we, who hardly even remembers where they live or how many children they have, suddenly be so presumptuous as to start to talk about their dead wife? What could possibly give us, who has forgotten their surname, the right to jump over our ignorance and rifle in the antechamber of their hearts with questions about their late father?

A commitment to authenticity ties us in knots. What could we possibly say with sincerity when we never knew the person who is gone? How can we proclaim to be sad about the death of someone we never till recently suspected ever lived?

Then we worry because there is so little time to handle the mourning properly. We are on our way to a conference room where a meeting is about to begin; or we only have until we reach the 12th floor of the office building. How can we shoehorn sympathy for a life that lasted many decades into the second before the lift doors open?

There is throughout an overarching fear that there's a very right but also a very wrong way to do this—and we don't know, or can't remember, the precise rules. Bereavement looms as a strict club, with distinctive rituals, language, and etiquette, into which we have never been properly inducted and therefore have no business straying. We haven't got a grip on the requisite stock of euphemisms. We dimly recall that we aren't under any circumstances to say "death"; only evasive words like "loss." We're meant to pull our face into a particular kind of sympathetic expression—but its nuances escape us. We have to put on an act that we haven't been trained for and don't have a script to.

There's also a panic that by touching on the issue, we'll open a faucet that can't be turned off. The acquaintance, who had only a minute ago been headed to lunch or home with a reasonably resolute manner, will—the minute we mention the issue—promptly be reminded of a ghastliness that they had narrowly managed to push to the back of their consciousness and fall into cataclysmic distress. Their face will freeze, they will let go of their bags and begin an anguished wail which will ring out across the public square or down the corridor to the open-plan office. We'll be nursing them for the next hour and a half at least; our jacket will be damp with their tears. It will be like picking up a cracked bowl and having it fall into a hundred pieces in our palm. No wonder we're going to walk very carefully around the perimeter of the park— or take the other exit out onto the street.

But none of these eventualities and scenarios holds true in practice. The risks are all on the other side, the side of scampering and silence. There is in reality no special club for the bereaved, it's simply a vast drafty stadium into which everyone will be herded soon enough. We don't have to pass an exam or have initiation rites. Someone we love just needs to wake up one morning complaining of a headache and suffer a stroke on the way to the bathroom—and a lifetime membership will be on its way.

The people who've lost their loved ones aren't different from us. They are us in a few years minus a very adored human. We don't therefore need to say any particular words or bow in an unusual way. We don't need to wrap things in velvet. "Sorry your gran died" will do; even "what a pisser" is OK if that's more generally your style. Death comes in vernacular forms as well; it's a "fucker" and a "bastard" as much as it's a "loss" or a "passing."

The bereaved don't expect sympathizers to stick around for hours; they don't have hours themselves. But a lot can be conveyed in two minutes. Some of the greatest poetry humans have ever written has expressed key sentiments in under that time.

It doesn't matter that we didn't know the grandma or the dad. We're not being asked to comment specifically on them, we're paying our respects to the pain of death in general.

The chances of the bereaved falling apart on us in the process are minuscule. They've been crying for days. They're getting the hang of the faucet, when it needs to be opened and how much by.

Death may be an enormous thing, but its scale never invalidates a role for small signs of care. We should find a few words in the hope that one day, when we're in the bereavement stadium, a near stranger will walk up to us and say something like, "Sorry about your dad," or "It must be really painful about your mum," and it won't be remotely insensitive and certainly won't set us off, but it will make us momentarily feel that we're not entirely alone with the worst thing that's yet happened to us, that acquaintances care a bit and that we all ultimately face the random tragic shitshow of death together.

14
How to Spill a Drink down Your Front—and Survive

It is, in many ways, the quintessential minor social mishap. We're at a party surrounded by interesting people upon whom we'd like to make a good impression. We've been talking about an aspect of our work or describing a small restaurant in Vietnam where we had lunch on a recent trip. Overall, it's going well. But we also earlier took a decision to have a red wine and, as we turn to say something to the person on our immediate right, now tip the contents of our glass over ourselves.

Everyone looks at us with a mixture of surprise, pity, and, perhaps, barely veiled contempt. We desperately try to dab ourselves, but it's obviously hopeless.

There's a huge sprawling red patch across our light-blue front and whatever we say or do now won't change a thing. Our identity will be fixed for the rest of the evening and possibly, in these people's eyes, for the rest of our lives. We are the nitwit who started an anecdote and ended up with what looks like a murder on their clothes. We are a buffoon. It's a great party but it's time to go to bed—and possibly never to leave home again.

At such moments of potential humiliation, the socially skilled person is armed with two intertwined consoling thoughts, one about themselves, the other about people in general. What helps them to remain calm and good-natured is that they have accepted, long ago, in less anguished circumstances, way before the glass tipped over them, that they are an idiot. They are an idiot now, they have been an idiot in the past, and they will be an idiot always. They are an idiot who spills drinks, who says the wrong things, who trips on unexpected steps, who turns off their computer by mistake, who loses hotel room keys, who gets in a muddle around dates and places, who underestimates how long journeys will take, and who tries to tell jokes but reveals the punchline too soon. It's extremely annoying, but it is not surprising and nor is it an affront to a carefully constructed ego or a heightened sense of dignity. The wise person lacks the furious, flustered, offended response of the haughty person brought low by their own momentary clumsiness—because they never had expectations of their own nobility to start with. Moments of idiocy do not shatter a pristine feeling of competence; they just confirm that they are fundamentally rather broken and imperfect, a thought that they have come to terms with from the outset, with grace and a touch of humor. The spilt red wine is not teaching the wise person anything they didn't know, it's merely confirming an essentially asinine nature that they have never overlooked for even an hour.

What helps to cushion the blow of this potentially harsh idea, and drain it of any self-persecutory dimension, is the knowledge that—fortunately—everyone else is an idiot too. The clumsy person's folly isn't a special curse, it's a universal feature of the human condition. The wine-spiller is not particularly cretinous because everyone else is—in some way or another—a total fool as well. Those who are present might look poised just now, but they must logically all have done many exceedingly ridiculous things in the past. At various unknown times, they've been utterly daft: they've made embarrassing noises; their voices came out at an odd high pitch; they've stood on the tail of their hosts' dog; they've discovered too late that there's no toilet paper in the bathroom; they've forgotten their own name ... Understanding the ubiquity of all this, the wise respond benevolently to the human comedy. They are implicit followers of Michel de Montaigne and his vital reminder: "To learn that we have said or done a stupid thing is nothing, we must learn a more ample and important lesson: that we are but blockheads ... On the highest throne in the world, we are seated, still, upon our arses."

The wise person escapes the worst ravages of social embarrassment by owning their mishaps with modesty. They tease themselves a long time before anyone else has a chance to do it for them. They are not terrified that a mocking impression of their character will form in the minds of their audiences, because they assume from the beginning that a bit of gentle mockery is what they deserve. The person who accepts that they are a bit of a fool need never fear that the world will one day discover they are such a thing—and humiliate them for it. Through their timely and mature reconciliation with their own mediocrity, they manage to win over all those who might otherwise be tempted to humble them—and end up charming the world, despite a very large stain down their front.

15
How to Deal with the Subtext

What stops many of our friendships from deepening is the background presence of a range of difficult but unspoken feelings that interrupt the growth of trust and the free flow of affection. Our friendships are shallower and more brittle than they might be because they are afflicted by a subtext: hampered by a layer of unresolved and unmentionable embarrassments, resentments, envious feelings, unreciprocated desires, hurts, and misunderstandings.

On being prompted, most of us are capable of scanning our friendships and quickly arriving at an idea of what the subtext might be in almost every example (rare is the friendship that lacks such a thing).

In one friendship, one of us fancied the other, it wasn't mutual, and both sides know it. In another, there's a jealousy that one person earns more than another and a suspicion that they've become grand and a show-off as a result. In a third, one of the parties feels they put in more effort and are taken for granted, while the other feels guilty but also penalized for circumstances beyond their control. In a fourth, there's a lingering anger over a dispute from five years ago. In a fifth, there was a birthday gathering that one of them gave that the other wasn't invited to and still can't forget.

The problem is that we are so well trained in the art of leaving subtexts alone—and of forgetting they are even there. Our childhoods subtly enforce the lesson that subtexts are not to be investigated and divulged. Rare are the parents who really want to know the contents of their children's trickier feelings, or the schools or fellow pupils who have the time or wherewithal to handle emotional complexities. The world of work is equally cautionary. Disparities in power, and the need to make the month's figures, generally put an end to any sustained investigation of background knots.

As a result, we carry our hurt in vague, unformulated, and disassociated forms. We may sense a degree of disappointment, of something not being quite right—but we haven't got the tools or the confidence to imagine there might be a better way. We're inclined to a basic, long-standing pessimism about what might be possible in human relationships.

Addressing the subtext adequately requires an unusual dose of hope and a newly minted strength of mind. For a start, and most importantly, it demands that we no longer feel ashamed for experiencing things that run counter to the notion of a problem-free, breezy friendship. It means accepting that we might be essentially good people and yet beset by troubling envy or resentment, guilt, or desire.

This impression of fundamental legitimacy about our feeling should then lead us to be calm and self-possessed in the way we eventually express ourselves. The danger is that we say nothing for too long and then, worried about our rights but unable to contain our anger, explode. Or that we become immensely tearful in our moments of confession in a way that fatally undermines our message. But with sufficient self-confidence, we can afford to be strategic—that is, guided by an understanding of what will best enable us to get through to someone. We will have a capacity to delay and temper our raw impulses in the name of success. We'll be able to employ an armory of tools: the right kind of humor; the deft, apparently throwaway, but extremely meaningful comment; the sincere but calm confession; the simultaneously vulnerable yet undesperate tone …

It is humbling, given how much time has already passed, how readily it might lie in our power, once we've done a little internal work, to start to resolve the harmful subtexts in our friendships. To one person, we might explain that though we always longed to be with them, we've now come to realize that we would have made them thoroughly miserable—and are therefore so grateful that they had the foresight (this needs to be said with a smile) to spare us both years of misery. To another friend, we might—as we pay the bill for a dinner we'd suggested—remark how sorry we are that we've found so little time to see them, but that it is nothing at all to do with being grand and full of oneself, merely too often afflicted by anxiety and exhaustion. We could at points dare to be emotionally very direct, to say how much someone means to us and how much we hope we're not intruding on them or how much we respect them or long to make amends to them. We might pre-empt the other's subtext by naming it for them ("I guess you might be thinking I'm a very bad person ...") or take on a bit of the blame as a way of teasing out a confession from the other party ("It might have been my fault for getting back so late ...").

Our friendships are so much poorer than they might be because we are dispiritingly passive in relation to the tensions that naturally develop between people. With counter-productive speed, we take ourselves to be too awful to complain, or too horrible to have dissenting feelings, or beyond pardon for having messed things up. We should dare to locate the subtext in our minds, to surmount our inhibiting shame and to bring things up the next time we meet our friends. We stand—thereby—to feel a great deal less scared, alone, and resentful.

16
How to Stop Worrying Whether or Not They Like You

One of the most acute questions we ask ourselves in relation to new friends and acquaintances is whether or not they like us. The question feels so significant because, depending on how we answer it in our minds, we will either take steps to deepen the friendship or, as is often the case, immediately make moves to withdraw from it so as to spare ourselves humiliation and embarrassment.

But what is striking and sad is how essentially passive we are in relation to this enquiry. We assume that there is a more or less binary answer, that it is wholly in the remit of the other person to settle it—and that there is nothing much we could do to shift the verdict one way or the other. Either someone wants to be our friend or they don't, and the answer, while it is about us, is essentially disconnected from any of our own initiatives.

We are hereby failing to apply to other people a basic lesson we can appreciate well enough when we study the functioning of our own judgments: We often don't know what we think of other people. Our moods hover and sway. There are days when we can see the point of someone and others when their positive sides elude us entirely. But, and this is the key point, what usually helps us to decide what someone means to us is our sense of what we mean to them.

The possibility of friendship between people therefore frequently hangs in the balance because both sides are, privately, waiting for a sign from the other one as to whether or not they are liked—before they dare to show (or even register) any enthusiasm of their own. Both sides proceed under the tacit assumption that there is some a priori verdict about their value that the other person will be developing in their mind that has no connection to how they themselves behave and is impervious to anything they could say or do.

Under pressure, we forget the fundamental malleability within the question of whether someone wants to be friends with us or not. Most of it depends on how we behave to them. If we have a little courage and can keep our deep suspicions of ourselves and our terror of their rejection of us at bay, we have every opportunity to turn the situation in our direction. We can dare to persuade them to see us in a positive light—chiefly by showing a great deal of evidence that we see them in a positive light. We can apply the full range of charming techniques: We can remember small things about them, display an interest in what they have been up to, laugh at their witty moments, and sympathize with them about their sorrows.

Though our instinct is to be close to superstitious in our understanding of why people like us, we have to be extremely unlucky to land on people who genuinely show no interest in a friendship with us once we have carried out a full set of charming maneuvers with any level of sincerity and basic tact.

Friendships cannot develop until one side takes a risk by showing they are ready to like even when there's as yet no evidence that they are liked back. We have to realize that whether or not the other person likes us is going to depend on what we do, not—mystically—on what we by nature "are," and that we have the agency to do rather a lot of things. Even though we may initially get very few signs of their interest (they might be looking a little distracted and behaving in an off-hand way), we should assume that this is only a legacy of a restraint that springs from fear that they are not able to please—and that so long as we keep showing them warmth and encouragement to appease their self-suspicion, the barriers will eventually come down.

It is sad enough when two people dislike each other. It is even sadder when two people fail to connect because both parties defensively but falsely guess that the other doesn't like them—and out of low self-worth, don't take any risk whatever to alter the situation. We should stop worrying quite so much whether or not people like us and do that far more interesting and socially useful move: concentrate on showing that we like them.

17
How to Be a Good Guest

It's normal to want to be a good guest; an intense wish to please tends to guide us when we accept a dinner invitation or spend a weekend with friends. And we generally fulfill this ambition by following a leading theory of what satisfies other humans: We mimic our hosts. We follow their lead in the conversation, we discuss what they want to discuss, we eat when they want to eat. We are malleable, we adjust; we laugh at pretty much anything they find funny.

It sounds extremely generous and deeply well-intentioned, but there's a strange aspect to this theory: the mimetic person is not, in practice, especially pleasing. They may not be offensive, but nor are they particularly memorable, interesting, or even likeable.

By contrast there is another social type who is a great deal more winning: the person who expresses their own distinctive needs with clarity while nevertheless remaining at all times gracious and socially vigilant. This more richly characterful person will, over dinner, remark with a smile that they happen to find the politician everyone is meant to hate oddly attractive, at least in fantasy. They tell us about an embarrassing thing that happened to them recently at work—or about a regret that haunts them in their emotional lives. When they are our house guest, they inform us in a rather precise though always highly polite way when they like to go to sleep, how much time they need on their own, and what their bathroom requirements are. They apologize for being a bit mad in a way that suggests profound sanity. They add that they'd deeply appreciate a boiled egg with biscuits for lunch. They are, in the best way, a bit peculiar.

It isn't that the mimetic person harms us; they simply don't reassure or endear us. A key part of what we seek in social contact is a feeling that our eccentricities and less-easily mentioned dimensions find an echo in another person. And yet all we see when we come closer to the conformist guest is our own reflection.

What truly charms is the person who manages to possess both a character and politeness. The archetype for this is the endearing 4-and-a-half-year-old child. They'll tell a near stranger their ideas about where squirrels go at night, what they like to put in their sandwiches, and their nickname for their elderly grandfather. We colloquially call this "cute" but it's perhaps something more serious than this implies: more pointedly, it's a relief from the customary pressure to standardize human nature and to say nothing that will sound too odd or flavored.

The small child is reminding us that the variegated surface of every personality—theirs, but by implication ours as well—could be put on display and, rather than hurt or offend, simply charm and enliven.

The good guest combines the candor of the child with the social empathy of the self-aware adult. They know how to be that rare and much prized social phenomenon: a loveable eccentric.

There is a sad background to the people-pleasing adult who doesn't in the end even please so much. They are generally the outcome of a style of parenting that didn't allow character or originality to show through. They had to hide who they really were for fear of upsetting an angry or vulnerable set of caregivers.

We cannot erase the past, but we can cease waging an active war on our characters in public. Our true selves may once have been unwanted, but it's only on the basis of being able to show them now that proper friendships can begin. Being merely polite is, in the end, an overly low ambition. We have exaggerated how much people like to be imitated and invariably agreed with. It is easy to tolerate such types, but very hard to love them. To truly please people requires that we dare to show a little more of the touching weirdness that lurks within us all.

18
How to Tell Someone They Have Spinach between Their Teeth

It is a classic minor moment of embarrassment through which we glimpse the largest, most touching themes of social existence: somewhere during the main course, a large, oblong forest-green piece of spinach has come to snag itself on one of the maxillary central incisors of the companion on our left and now lends them an almost clownish or rogue-like expression, of which they are utterly and painfully oblivious.

The spinach is an emblem for how lightly life can mock us and frustrate our plans for dignity and adult competence. We are never more than an open fly or a laddered stocking away from absurdity.

As an observer, we are liable to be torn between

an obligation to spare our companion further embarrassment in front of other witnesses and a fear that we will in some ways be shot, or at least take some shrapnel, as the messengers of profoundly awkward news.

Successfully navigating the risks relies on holding in mind a critical distinction between pity on the one hand and sympathy on the other—and ensuring that we dispense plenty of the latter while fending off so much as a hint of the former.

Both pity and sympathy are responses to sorrow in another person, but pity implies that the sorrow before us is of a kind from which we ourselves are and always will be immune—while sympathy is built out of a sincerely held, shared sense of human error and misery. As pitying people, we may feel very bad for our companion, but we also know—and imply—that we haven't been there, and realistically never will. Pity is what a medieval monarch would have felt for a gangrenous peasant, or what the most popular and attractive person at school might feel for the acned nerd.

Sympathy, on the other hand, implicates a witness in tune to the suffering of another: their pain has been, currently is, or could one day very plausibly be our own. We extend our kindness knowing that we are exposed to comparable misfortunes. We are the superiors of those we pity, but the committed equals of those we sympathize with.

There are generally only minute differences between the ways we express pity and sympathy: a slight change in tone, a subtle emphasis in the eyes, or movement in the lips. Nevertheless, the effect on the recipient can be immense. The sympathetic person leaves their spinach-toothed companion in no doubt that they have suffered comparable mishaps a hundred times before. There is nothing cursed or damned about this, nothing regrettable or worth hating oneself for. Life is humiliating for everyone— and the best response to setbacks is simply warm fellow feeling and laughter. The sympathetic person remembers their own troubled and sometimes very unimpressive history and always brings it to bear on the mishaps and sorrows of others. Today they might be able to manage comfortably, but at various times, they too have been in chaos, and are sure to be so again before too long. The sympathetic person knows that all kinds of weaknesses are compatible with being loveable. It is normal and wholly unsurprising to feel shy, to be ignorant of certain social conventions, to be preoccupied, to have made grave errors—and to have a large bit of spinach in your teeth.

The pitying person, on the other hand, quietly crushes us by implying that truly competent adults don't mess up. They imply a race, to which they belong, of self-contained, poised, wholly serene beings who don't crave reassurance, encouragement, compliments, assistance, or forgiveness, who don't wake up in the night in terror or walk into doors on leaving important meetings.

The sighting of the spinach is a call to friendship. We should imply to our companions that this flaw is nothing next to the mess in our souls, that we are every bit as damaged and frail as they are and, in fact, a good deal more so. We must leave them in no doubt that we like them a lot, not because they are perfect, but precisely because—thank goodness—they so absolutely aren't.

19
How to Make People Feel Good about Themselves

We tend to operate with the view that the best way to please people is not to bother them too much. We keep many of our dilemmas and confusions away from those we like, for fear of irritating or inconveniencing them and so spoiling the relationship. We may well have a voice echoing in our minds from childhood: "Don't bother your mother, can't you see she's exhausted from her trip?" "Don't bother your father, he works hard for us and he's busy right now." There are powerful reasons why we equate making others happy with burdening them as little as possible.

But our analysis is missing a key detail of human psychology: We like to be bothered. Not at all times and over all things, nor at the expense of our own critical needs, but fundamentally, we have a powerful urge to feel helpful. We need to be needed. All of us suffer from a fear of superfluity, which the requirements of others has a critical capacity to appease. However nice presents may be for our friends, the real gift we can offer them is an insight into our problems.

We can pick this theme up in the realm of work. The dominant societal story is that we work strictly for ourselves: for our status and our financial benefit. But in reality, more puzzlingly but far more beautifully, what really makes our work feel exciting and meaningful is the power it gives us to help other people. Work is at its most gratifying when it affords us a feeling that we have, over the course of the day, managed to appease the suffering or increase the pleasure of another person. There are so many stories of being exhausted by the requests of others; too few of the delight we experience when we turn around someone else's distress, boredom, or craving. We can't ultimately feel our valuable sides until we are called upon to exercise them: We don't have a sense of our strength until someone needs us to lift something; we can't feel intelligent until someone asks us to solve an issue; we can't feel wise until we've been brought in to adjudicate a dispute. We rely on the needs of others to remind us what we're capable of.

What holds true in professional life applies as much to personal experience. The best way to charm and break the ice with a new person we like the look of in a public place isn't to try to say something witty or soothing. We should strive to bring them a question. We should ask them whether we're in the right queue; whether they know when the post office opens—or if they have any idea how long a chicken this size might need in the oven.

With closer friends, too, we should dare to reveal our bemusements. We should ask them if they could possibly spare a moment, then solicit their views on what we might do about our angry teenager, how we should cope with a less than sexually fulfilling relationship, or how we might better handle a colleague prone to panic. Our questions will indicate how ready we are to make ourselves vulnerable in their eyes—and therefore how wise and kind we must take them to be.

This isn't just a cynical strategy for ingratiating ourselves; it isn't Machiavellian or sly. We aren't pretending to have problems and making a few up to flatter. We are suffering inside, but generally don't dare to reveal the truth for fear of driving people away. And yet we are staying guarded out of an ideal of self-sufficiency that isn't either true to our needs or constructive for the well-being and esteem of others.

We should risk doing what we at heart have always longed to do: to reveal some of the fear, sadness, and angst we genuinely feel to those who seem to care about us. We will be helped in our pain, we will remind others of their capacities—and, if we are fortunate, we'll set a precedent that means that others will one day bring a few of their problems to us in turn.

20
How to Face Social Catastrophe

We try so hard to do it right: we are polite, we apologize, we write thank you letters, we ask people how their day was, we bring cake.

And yet, whatever our efforts, nothing will spare us occasional involvement in the sort of outright social calamity that we know, even as it unfolds, is going to sear itself into our memories and be written in indelible ink across our lives.

We might be at a drinks party where we mention how much we enjoyed reading a very funny, very scathing review of a new book. Then someone whispers to us that one of the people we are addressing is the book's author.

Or we were instrumental in having a particular colleague fired—and now they are at the next table in the little restaurant and have looked up and noticed us.

Or our partner left their devastated spouse for us a year ago, and now this spouse is next to us in line at the airport, waiting to board the same flight.

Or we notice a heavily pregnant woman standing near us on a train and offer her our seat. She thanks us and, with a wan smile, specifies that she isn't pregnant at all.

We have not set out to be evil or idiotic—the book really was very badly written, our colleague was truly not suited to the role, our partner is much happier with us, the passenger did legitimately look close to their due date—and yet we have unleashed what is without question a disaster.

One way of reacting is to apologize profusely, then to try to explain, in a lot of detail perhaps, why things are in fact OK. We strive to restore a good impression of us in the other's mind and to repair the violently torn social fabric. We give reasons why we might be misunderstood or have made a slip. We rehearse the failings of the book but add that in many ways it was lovely too, especially in the later chapters; we explain that there was nothing personal in the sacking, it was a collective decision based purely on objective considerations; or we evolve a theory of relationships in which there is no ownership of partners; or start to describe how the cut of their overcoat in that particular position reasonably suggested the outline of a growing infant …

But there might be another, better way, one in which we accept—with immense dignified stoic pessimism and a sense of dark and gigantic responsibility—that there is simply nothing we can do other than fall silent and absorb our failure and the mismatch between who we are and the direction of the universe. We recognize that any shred of politeness will now lie on the side of leaving things broken, that anything else will be sentimentality and self-serving blather. We give up our pretense of being a wholly kind or ethical person and reckon with our awesome powers to inflict wrong. Our name will always be a byword for insensitivity and idiocy in certain circles and we will have to carry the pain in our hearts until the end. We will be wincing decades from now at the irredeemable proof of a stubborn strain of cowardice and foolishness within us.

Oddly, this kind of clear-eyed self-criticism is not without its uses. It is the necessary foundation for a less blithe and presumptuous, more ethical and more careful future. We will henceforth better understand how easily we can damage other people, how unwittingly we can inflict pain, how tragic the mismatch can be between intentions and effect—and from such an awareness will spring ever greater efforts to be, wherever possible, a bit more gentle, tolerant, forgiving, darkly funny, uncomplaining, and unself-righteous. Our moments of social catastrophe will reinforce our always fragile but deeply necessary commitment to a life of self-examination, kindness, and good manners.

Picture credits

- 10 Keystone / Stringer / Getty Images
- 16 © Martin Parr / Magnum Photos
- 22 Julian Kevin Zakaras / Fairfax Media Archives / Contributor / Getty Images
- 28 Adam Scull / Shutterstock
- 32 Rose Hartman / Contributor / Getty Images
- 35 John Constable, *Cloud Study: Stormy Sunset*, 1821-1822. Oil on paper on canvas, 20.3 x 27.3 cm. Accession Number 1998.20.1. Gift of Louise Mellon in honour of Mr. and Mrs. Paul Mellon. Courtesy National Gallery of Art, Washington
- 38 Fairchild Archive / Penske Media / Shutterstock
- 44 Richard E. Aaron / Contributor / Getty Images
- 48 George Rose / Contributor / Getty Images
- 54 Fairchild Archive / Penske Media / Shutterstock
- 60 Central Press / Stringer / Getty Images
- 64 Des Moines Art Center, Des Moines, Iowa, USA / De Agostini Picture Library / Bridgeman Images © Heirs of Josephine Hopper / Licensed by Artists Rights Society (ARS) NY DACS, London 2019
- 66 Central Press / Stringer / Getty Images
- 72 Zuma / Shutterstock
- 76 Jeanette Jones / Shutterstock
- 82 Fairchild Archive / Penske Media / Shutterstock
- 88 Fairchild Archive / Penske Media / Shutterstock
- 94 Central Press / Stringer / Getty Images
- 100 Fox Photos / Stringer / Getty Images
- 106 Chris Barham / Associated Newspapers / Shutterstock
- 112 Roger-Viollet / Shutterstock
- 118 Keystone / Staff / Getty Images

Also available from The School of Life:

The School of Life: On Being Nice
A guide to friendship and connection

A guide to rediscovering niceness as one of the highest of all human achievements.

Most books that want to change us seek to make us richer or thinner. This book wants to help us to be nicer: that is, less irritable, more patient, readier to listen, warmer, less prickly ... Niceness may not have the immediate allure of money or fame, but it is a hugely important quality nevertheless and one that we neglect at our peril.

This is a guide to the uncharted landscape of niceness, gently leading us around the key themes of this forgotten quality. We learn how to be charitable, how to forgive, how to be natural, and how to reassure. We learn that niceness is compatible with strength and is no indicator of naivety. Niceness deserves to be rediscovered as one of the highest of all human achievements.

UK ISBN: 978-1-915087-02-7 / US ISBN: 978-1-915087-15-7